SERVICECRAFT

TABLE SERVICE WORKBOOK

Holly Bamunuge
and David Karet
Birmingham College of Food Technology

Series Editor: Roy Hayter, Hotel and Catering Training Board

MACMILLAN

First published 1988

Published by
MACMILLAN EDUCATION LTD
Houndmills, Basingstoke, Hampshire RG21 2XS
and London
Companies and representatives
throughout the world

Printed in Great Britain by
Scotprint Ltd, Musselburgh

ISBN 0–333–46336–6

CONTENTS

ACKNOWLEDGEMENTS

The publishers would like to thank sincerely the following for their help with the photographs and illustrations used in this book:

Barclays Banks (unit 16)
Catherine Blackie (picture research)
Anthony Blake Photo Library (Capital Hotel) (unit 12)
Brook Hotel, Felixstowe (unit 18, photographer Edward Morgan, shows Alexandra Boyd who plays Gizzi in the Customercraft video)
Crest Hotels (units 14 and 15)
Grand Metropolitan Retailing (unit 2)
London Tara Hotel, Kensington (units 4 and 19, photographer Catherine Blackie)
Mecca Leisure Group plc (units 5 and 17)
Thistle Hotels (unit 9)
Travellers Fare (unit 8)
The White House Restaurant, Regents Park, London (unit 3, photographer Alexia Cross)

The publishers are grateful for the major contribution made by Jennifer Kimber (freelance writer), Mary James and Gill Verstage to the final text of this book.

The aims of the book

This book is concerned with the basic procedures involved in serving food and drink to customers at the table. Self-service forms of service—in other words where the customers leave the table to collect the food, or proceed to the table having collected the food—are dealt with in the companion title *Servicecraft: Counter Service Workbook*. A third title, *Servicecraft: Food and Beverage Service*, deals comprehensively with the theory and takes many of the issues explored in this Workbook to greater depth.

The emphasis in this Workbook is quite simply that customers' needs come first. This is the emphasis throughout the Mastercraft books and in the supporting videos, particularly *Servicecraft 1: Table Service* and *Customercraft: Keeping the Customers Satisfied*. Hotel and catering establishments exist to provide a service to their customers. It makes little difference whether they are in a restaurant, hotel, pub or leisure centre, at school or college, in hospital or an old person's home, or whether the aim of the service is to make a profit (which will only happen if customers come in sufficient numbers) or to meet budgets laid down by a national or local authority.

How the book works

Servicecraft: Table Service Workbook is designed in units of work laid out on each double page spread. Taking core facts and know-how as its points of departure, each spread moves out towards

- application of skills in the workplace
- interesting and useful detail
- reflective points and reminders.

Every unit includes an activity TO DO, intended to help the reader gain a better understanding and more personal experience of the topics covered.

The structure of the book

The first unit looks briefly at the customers in food service. The two Insight units introduce the activities common to all styles of service and look at the fundamental questions of food presentation and appearance.

Units 4 to 16 are all concerned with the 'how to', for the aim of the Mastercraft Workbooks is to help the reader in his or her day-to-day activities.

With so many establishments now following a mixed-style of service—one based on meeting the needs of their customers rather than a particular traditional style—it has been felt important to deal in these Method units with the procedures in such a way that they can be applied to a variety of meal situations in a wide variety of establishments. There is no distinction made between the service of lunch or (evening) dinner, for example.

Those readers who are seeking Caterbase food and beverage qualifications for the skills they use in their job on a day-to-day basis, or for new skills they wish to acquire, will therefore find the book of direct assistance.

It will also help students studying for City and Guilds and SCOTVEC qualifications in food and beverage service.

The personal side of service is returned to in the two Customercraft units, 17 and 18. The final units deal with working efficiently, safely and hygienically.

1 THE CUSTOMER

Food service customers may be divided into three groups: those who are able and can afford to eat out, those who have no choice where to eat and, possibly, what to eat, and those who are relatively limited in their choice. The amount of choice will affect where the customer will eat.

Where do customers eat?

1. Customers who can choose where to eat The type of restaurant chosen may be a high class restaurant, a coffee shop, a fast food burger bar, a wine bar or a speciality food restaurant. The choice of outlet will depend on:

- The *time* available to the customer.
- How much *money* the customer is prepared to spend.
- The *reason* for the meal, for example, whether the meal is a special celebration, a business lunch or a snack while carrying out some other activity such as shopping.
- How *far* the customer is prepared to travel.
- The customers' *food preference*—the type of food they wish to eat, for example, Indian food or a pizza.
- What *atmosphere* is desired—a quiet dinner for two or a lively cabaret show during the meal.
- The *time of day* – this will influence the choice in that many restaurants are only open for limited periods.
- *Familiarity* or *personal recommendation*—if a customer has a particular favourite restaurant, then there may be no reason to consider any other option.

2. Customers who have no choice where to eat These include:

- children at school
- hospital patients
- meals-on-wheels customers
- prisoners
- people working away from home, such as on an oil rig.

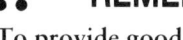

> **‼ REMEMBER**
>
> **To provide good service you should:**
>
> Smile and be friendly.
>
> Establish eye contact.
>
> Use the customer's name.
>
> Show you respect and accept the customer, regardless of race, colour, class etc.
>
> Know and understand the menu, cooking terms and times, and wines.
>
> Give customers your undivided attention.
>
> Demonstrate respect for your colleagues and your employer.
>
> Show skill and efficiency when serving.
>
> Be calm and confident.
>
> Make a good impression on the customers by presenting a clean and pleasant appearance.

3. Customers who have a limited choice where to eat

- Train passengers may use the train buffet facilities, the station food outlets, bring their own food with them or wait until they reach their destination.
- Car travellers are slightly freer, but may be unwilling to travel far from their route to find refreshment. On a motorway, the most convenient eating option will be the motorway service station.

What do food service customers expect?

When people are eating away from home, how satisfied they are with the food and service they receive depends on the following.

1. The quality of the food   Wherever the customers are eating they will have certain expectations of the food they are ordering, these include:

- a certain quality of product
- well prepared food, which looks and tastes good
- hot food served hot, cold food served cold.

2. Value for money   Whether the establishment is a high class restaurant or a fish and chip shop, the customers' satisfaction with what they receive will depend to some extent on the prices they are charged. The value expected will vary from one customer to another, but generally all customers will want to feel that they have had their money's worth.

3. Pleasant surroundings   The physical environment of the restaurant, which is influenced by:

- the decor, including the furniture, lighting, and music
- the cleanliness and standards of hygiene

is one factor in producing the expected environment for the customers. Another, equally important factor is the quality of service.

4. The quality of service   The level of service expected will depend partly on the price the customers are paying, on what they have received in other restaurants, and even on their mood. Generally if it is:

- attentive and efficient but not rushed
- friendly and welcoming, but not too familiar
- helpful, especially in advising on the selection of food and beverage

then their expectations will be met.

See: Servicecraft videos.

How can customer expectations be met by the serving staff?

The members of serving staff are in effect selling the food, beverages and services of the establishment. They are involved in helping to create a pleasant and appropriate atmosphere, mainly by finding out what the customer needs and wants and providing it.

Types of food service

Basically food service can be divided into two groups:

1. **Table service**, where food is brought to the customers.
2. **Counter service**, where the customers collect their own food.

 TO DO

Carry out a survey among a small group of your friends or colleagues: ask about the occasions when they have eaten a meal away from home in the last seven days (or a longer period if you wish). Where did they choose to eat? What was the reason for their choice? How far did they go to get the meal? What sort of food did they eat? What time of day was it?

The basic aim of table service is to bring food to the customers, and the way this is done will vary according to the type of restaurant. Whatever the style of service, there are certain common activities that must be carried out by the serving staff.

1. Preparing for service   In some restaurants the serving staff will be responsible for ensuring that the dining area is clean, that dirty linen has been removed from the restaurant for laundering and that all equipment is in a clean, hygienic state ready for service, and not chipped or otherwise damaged.

2. Laying tables   When the restaurant is in a clean and tidy condition, the serving staff will need to prepare the tables and sideboards (if these are used) for serving customers. The actual cutlery and crockery that is laid on the table will vary according to the type of menu that is on offer, for example, whether *à la carte* or *table d'hôte*.

3. Meeting, greeting, seating   When the customers arrive, the serving staff will be responsible for making them feel welcome, showing them to a table, taking coats, pulling chairs out for women or elderly customers and ensuring that any special needs are taken care of, for example, cushions or a high chair for a child.

4. Presenting the menu and taking orders   Once the customers are seated at the table the serving staff will present the menu, immediately taking any orders for aperitifs, and leave the customers for a while to make their choice. At this stage the customers may wish to seek advice from the serving staff on particular terms on the menu or on which wine to choose. The choices of the customers should be carefully recorded and taken to the kitchen so that the food may be prepared.

5. Serving the food   The way in which the food is brought to the customer will vary according to the type of establishment—whether high class hotel or small wine bar. In recent years the trend has been towards a more casual type of service, apart from in very high class establishments.

	Type of service	Examples of use
Plate	The food is assembled in the kitchen on plates	High class restaurants, guesthouses, set menus, breakfast
Silver or English	Food is transferred to the plate in front of the customer from a flat or serving dish, using a spoon and fork or other appropriate utensils such as a ladle	High class hotels, directors' dining room, functions
Family	The food is placed on the table in serving dishes, and the customers serve themselves	Indian and other ethnic restaurants
Mixed	The main item is plated and the vegetables are placed on the table in dishes for the customers to serve themselves, or silver served	Banquets, clubs
French or butler	The customers serve themselves from flats or dishes held at their side by the serving staff	Small banquets, royal functions
Russian	Similar to silver, each dish is presented, then transferred from the flat to the customer's plate at a side table or the sideboard	Small functions and private parties
Guéridon	Carving meat joints, boning or filleting fish, cooking whole dishes at a side table or trolley and transferring the food to the customer's plate at the side table. Sometimes 'guéridon' may be used to include plating the food at a side table	High class restaurants, night clubs

6. Serving wine and other beverages   Although some high class restaurants will employ a wine waiter, in most small establishments the food service staff will also serve the wine, and any other beverages.

7. Clearing the table   The serving staff will need to clear the table between courses, removing dirty plates, cutlery and glasses, and adjusting the place setting for the different dishes to be eaten.

8. Bringing the bill   In some small establishments the food service staff may be responsible for making up the customers' bills, or a cashier may be employed to carry out this function. However the serving staff must still ensure that all the items of food and drink that the customer has had are noted on the bill.

9. Taking payment   Once the customer has received the bill and checked through it, the serving staff will take the payment (cash, cheque, credit card or account) and bring back the receipt and change if appropriate.

10. Helping with coats   When payment has been received the serving staff should ensure that any coats are brought to the customers, and generally help them to leave the establishment in a way that will make them feel they would like to return.

  TO DO

For three restaurants in your locality find out as much as you can about the styles of service used.
   Make notes under the following headings:

1. Styles of service.
2. Food and beverages on offer.
3. Number of staff employed.
4. How many customers can be served in one session.

Presentation of food

The presentation and appearance of food is one of the most important aspects influencing customers' enjoyment of the meal.

Both the chef and the serving staff have the opportunity to show off their skills in food presentation. For example:

- The chef, by placing the food on the plate or serving dish to show contrasting colours and textures and attractive methods of decoration.
- The serving staff, by carrying and handling plates and equipment to create a sense of ceremony.

Serving attractive food is largely a matter of being neat and careful and using common sense. Effective and attractive food presentation also depends on the balance and arrangement of the food on the plate, and on the effectiveness of any decoration or garnishes which are used (see unit 9).

See: Counter Service video.

1. Balance

Colour— two or three colours on a plate are usually more interesting than one; a garnish of a fresh sprig of parsley may brighten an otherwise uninteresting dish.

Shape— a variety of shapes, for example, whole green beans with slices of meat add interest to the plate.

Texture—not strictly a visual consideration, but good balance requires a variety.

Flavour—is also a factor to be considered.

2. Portion size

- Match portion sizes and plates; an overcrowded plate looks messy, too large a plate makes the portion look mean.
- Balance the different items, don't let the main item get lost in a huge mound of vegetables.

 **TO DO**

Choose five hot or cold dishes served in your workplace (or on display in a local restaurant offering a buffet or self-service counter) that you consider to be attractively presented. Note why you think the dishes look attractive and what has been done to create the pleasing effect: colour, shape, choice of garnish etc.

3. Arrangement on the plate

- Keep food off the rim.
- Arrange the items for the convenience of the customer.
- Keep space between the items.
- Ensure the plate looks like one meal and not several unrelated items.
- Make the garnish count.
- Don't drown the food in sauce or gravy.
- Keep it simple.

Garnishing

The garnish is the decoration that is placed on the dish, usually once cooking has been completed.

- Many dishes need no garnish. If the accompanying vegetables provide an attractive balance and colour combination, the garnish may just clutter it up.
- Garnishes may be uncooked, or cooked. Cooked garnishes are usually served as accompaniments or side dishes.

When accompanying vegetables are served in side dishes or when the accompaniments do not provide much contrast to the plate, for example steak and a baked potato, a simple garnish may be necessary to provide colour or balance to the plate. This should be:

- edible
- appropriate to the food
- part of the plate layout, not stuck on haphazardly.

USEFUL TERMS

Some classical garnishes

Bouquetière—'bouquet' of vegetables
Jardinière—'garden' vegetables
Primeurs—first spring vegetables } (these terms all refer to assortments of fresh vegetables, including carrots, turnips, peas, green beans, cauliflower, and asparagus)

Clamart—peas
Dubarry—cauliflower
Florentine—spinach
Forestière—mushrooms
Lyonnaise—onions
Princesse—asparagus
Provençale—tomatoes, with garlic, parsley, and sometimes mushrooms and/or olives
Vichy—carrots

❚❙ SERVICE TIPS

Position of the food on the plate

1. If the plate has the restaurant's name or crest engraved on it, this should be at the top of the plate when it is placed in front of the customer, at a 12 o'clock position.
2. The main food item, fish or meat, should be at the bottom of the plate, near to the customer, in a 6 o'clock position.
3. Portions of sweet, which are triangular in shape, should be placed with the point towards the customer.

Creating the right environment in the restaurant is a vital part of the preparation procedure; this includes such factors as temperature, lighting and equipment. The physical atmosphere of the restaurant will influence whether or not the customer feels comfortable.

Opening duties

1. Make sure the dining room *temperature* is comfortable.
2. Check the level of *lighting*; this will depend on the particular establishment and the type of atmosphere it is trying to produce. Check light bulbs.
3. Make sure any *pictures* are hanging straight.
4. Check *chair* and *table positions*.
5. Check that all *china, glassware* and *cutlery* are clean and polished, and free from chips, cracks and other damage.
6. Inspect the dining room for *cleanliness* and *safety*. Check the condition of the toilets.
7. Make sure the *music* is organised and at the right noise level.
8. Check *reservations*; plan seating arrangements.
9. Check that the *menus* are available and in good condition.
10. Check the *menu items* and any changes.

Covering the table

The table provides the framework for laying-up.

Some restaurants use dining tables covered with cloths, others use polished tables on which plates are placed with or without table mats.

1. Setting a table with a tablecloth

- Handle the cloth as little as possible to avoid creasing or marking it.
- Ensure it is laid centrally, so that the points hang equally over the legs.
- An appropriate sized cloth should be used for each table, so that the cloth does not drag on the floor but covers the table adequately.
- When changing a cloth during service, the top of the table should not be shown.
- 'Slip' cloths may be used, these are small cloths which lie over the main table cloth, protecting it and thus saving on laundry.

2. Setting a table with place mats

- Ensure the table is clean and smear free.
- Place the mats 1.25 to 2.5 cm (½ to 1 inch) from the table edge, squarely in front of each chair.

When all the cloths or place mats have been laid, the crockery and cutlery should be laid.

Laying the tables

The serving staff may be required to lay the tables for breakfast, afternoon tea, a table d'hôte menu or an à la carte menu.

Table d'hôte   Each place setting will require:

- 8 pieces of cutlery (or whatever is required for the menu)
- a cover plate (this is a show plate and is not always used)
- a side plate
- a wine glass (up to three glasses may be laid, 2 types of wine glass, 1 water glass)
- a napkin
- one cruet set (salt and pepper) per table.

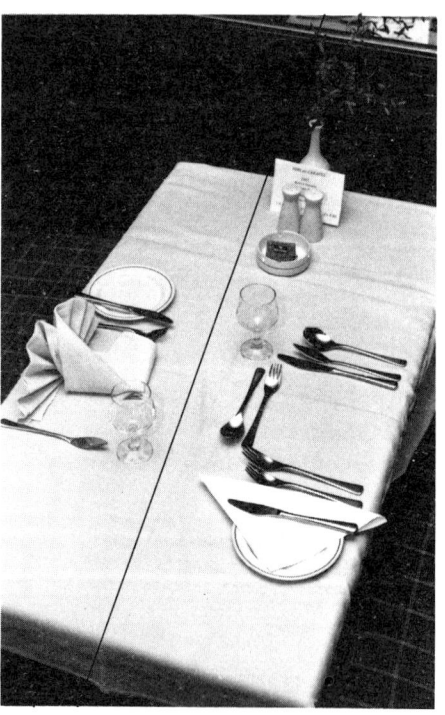

À la carte and Table d'hôte place settings

À la carte   Each place setting will require:

- 3 pieces of cutlery
- 1 side plate
- 1 glass
- a cover plate (if used)
- a napkin.

Other cutlery is brought to the table on a napkin-covered service plate, once the customer has ordered.

Laying-up procedure

1. Assemble all the necessary cutlery and crockery, cleaned and polished.
2. Place the cover plate (if used) 1.25 cm from the edge of the table, in a central position before each customer's chair. This makes it easier to lay the cutlery in the correct position.
3. Lay the cutlery from the inside, so that cutlery which is to be used first during the meal lies on the outside of the place setting.
4. Place the side plate to the left of the place setting.
5. Place the side knife on the plate.
6. Place the glass to the top right of the place setting, above the tip of the meat knife if laying table d'hôte.
7. Place a folded napkin on the cover plate, the side plate or in the glass according to the style of the restaurant.
8. Place the cruet on the table.

Completing the table   Everything should be clean and laid symmetrically. For example, looking down the length of a long table, this means all the glasses and napkins will be in a straight line; on a round table they will all be the same distance from the centre.

For tables of two or four, place the cruet and flowers (if available) centrally. For tables of three, use these items to balance the table but in a readily accessible position.

Ashtrays   It is usual nowadays to keep clean ashtrays on the side and bring them to the tables when it is apparent that customers wish to smoke.

This unit will help you gain the Caterbase module *Preparing for Restaurant Service*.

5 METHOD

Presenting the menu

Once the customers are seated, they should be handed the menu, open and the correct way up.

It is important to give the customers time to make their choices, while not appearing to abandon them.

Understanding the menu

The serving staff should have a good knowledge of the menu so that any customer queries can be answered. The serving staff should know:

1. The ingredients and description of each dish on the menu.
2. How each dish has been prepared and how it is to be served.
3. Any additions or alterations to the menu, such as the dish of the day.
4. If any items are unavailable.

Taking the order

There are three main ordering or 'checking' systems used in restaurants:

- Duplicate—making an extra copy of the order ⎫ with self-carbonated
- Triplicate—making two extra copies of the order ⎭ paper or by using a sheet of carbon paper

- Computerised—copies of the order are processed electronically from one terminal to all other departments requiring the information.

Whichever system is used in the restaurant, accurate details of the order must go to:

1. the kitchen, so that the food can be prepared for the customer
2. the cashier, so that the food is charged for on the customer's bill (see unit 16).

The first order taken will be for the starters and the main course, including any vegetables. Orders for desserts, coffees any other items are made on separate sheets.

What should be recorded on the order?

- Table number
- Number of customers to be served
- Date
- Server's initials or code number
- Details of the order, clearly written.

10

Points to note when taking orders

- Make sure the customers are ready to order, if they are not, leave the table and return in a few minutes.
- A plan of the table may help in remembering which customer orders which dish. Alternatively a note by each dish to help remind you, for example 'red suit'.
- Take orders from female customers first.
- Write figures clearly on the order, in advance of the name of the dish.
- If carbon paper is used in the order pad, make sure it is correctly placed.
- Draw a line between orders for starters and for main courses.
- Use the same name for the dish as that used on the menu.
- Make a clear note of any special requirements, such as how a steak should be cooked.
- Check that you have recorded all the orders, by ensuring the number of starters and main courses ordered agree with the number of customers.
- Always ensure that it is possible to supply a request before accepting it, for example, meat without sauce.
- Read back the order to the customers to confirm details.

Adjusting the cutlery

Once the customer's order has been taken, the serving staff should adjust the cutlery, if necessary. This ensures that customers have the correct cutlery to eat the dishes they have ordered.

Remove unwanted cutlery before placing new items in position.

Adjust the cutlery for both the starter and the main course.

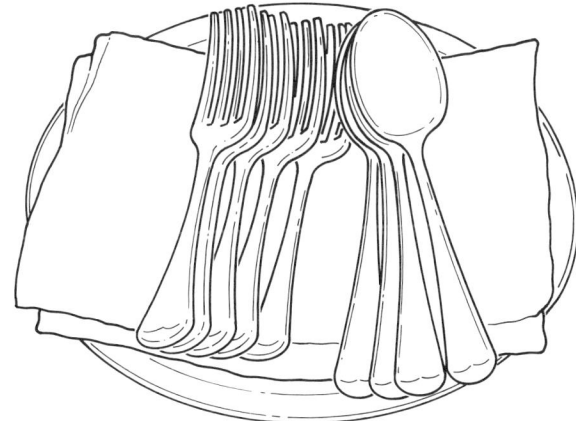

Any cutlery or other items brought to or removed from the table should be placed on a napkin-covered plate or salver

Examples of cutlery for starters

- Fish knife and fish fork—for any starter containing fish that needs to be eaten with a knife and fork, such as smoked trout.
- Fish fork and teaspoon—for dishes containing small pieces of fish, such as prawn cocktail.
- Sweet spoon and sweet fork—for a fruit starter that is in large pieces, such as melon boat, or for a pasta dish, when the spoon is placed on the right, the fork on the left.
- Sweet fork and teaspoon—for a fruit starter that is in small pieces, such as fruit cocktail.
- Side knife and sweet fork—for meat/savoury items that require cutting.

 SERVICE TIP

When removing cutlery from the table, serving staff should move round the table in one direction, taking the fork from the place setting of the customer on the right, at the same time removing the knife or spoon from the place setting of the customer on the left, if possible avoiding coming between two customers who are engaged in conversation.

▶ ▶ ▶ **TO DO**

Choose six dishes from the menu at your place of work or from a restaurant of your choice. Write a brief description of the ingredients and description of each dish, how it is prepared and how it is served.

The information in units 7 to 11 will help gain the Caterbase module *Taking Orders for Restaurant Service.*

6 METHOD

Collecting and serving the food

1. Take a copy of the order to the kitchen to ensure that the correct food is prepared.
2. Gather together sufficient serving spoons and forks (not required if all the food is served plated).
3. When *silver service* is being used:
   - Collect clean plates, which should be at the correct temperature, hot plates for hot food, cold plates for cold food.
   - Assemble on the sideboard, if there is one, or take straight to the table.
   - Place the plates in front of the customers.
   - Serve the food.
4. When *plate service* is being used, place the plates directly in front of the customers. If necessary assemble them on the sideboard, for example, because the service is to be co-ordinated (all the plates placed down at the same time, one member of waiting staff per customer).
5. Place the appropriate accompaniments on the table or serve them to the customers.
6. If some of the customers have ordered cold dishes, bring them to the table or sideboard before collecting any hot food.
7. Serve hot food as quickly as possible. This will mean judging carefully when to collect it from the kitchen (see unit 19).
8. Serve the main item of the course first, for example, meat before vegetables.

Sides for service

There are certain conventions on which side to serve different items to a customer. These should by no means be seen as *rules*; serving staff will on occasions have to use their own initiative as to which is the appropriate side, or a restaurant will observe its own house rules.

The most important rule to observe is that food should be served to customers from the side causing the least disturbance. Whichever side is used, it is important to be consistent to avoid confusing the customer.

1. **English conventions**
   - Plates or utensils for food are placed from the left.
   - Food is served from the left.
   - Used food plates are cleared from the left.
   - Glasses are placed from the right.
   - Drinks are served from the right.
   - Used glasses are cleared from the right.

This ensures that serving staff do not prevent customers from drinking while the food is being placed in front of them.

2. **Continental conventions**
   - Clean plates and glasses are placed from the right.
   - Coffee cups and saucers are placed from the left.
   - Food is served from the left.
   - Drinks are served from the right.
   - All used items are cleared from the right.

> **‼ REMEMBER**
>
> **Be prepared to adapt** Food serving techniques and procedures have developed for convenience, both in meeting customers' needs and in aiding service staff to operate efficiently.
>
> None of the methods discussed should be taken as *rules* nor should they be ignored; most restaurants adapt the methods to their individual requirements and convenience.

Placing the plates in front of the customer

Silver service

- Hold the pile of plates resting on the palm of the left hand. The palm is covered with one end of a serving cloth, the cloth wrapped around and over the top of the pile.

- On approaching the appropriate side of the customer, wipe the top plate with the end of the cloth, then pick up the plate with the tips of the thumb and fingers of the right hand.

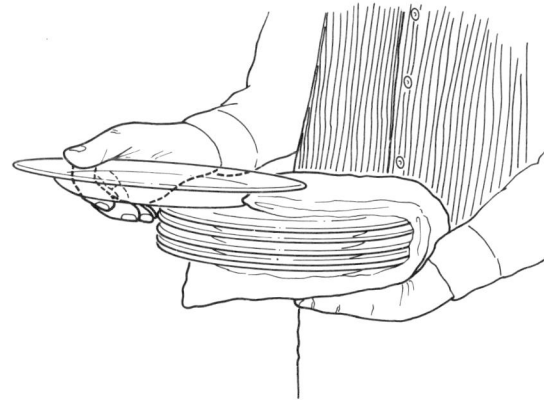

All types of service

- Keeping the plate horizontal, lean forward slightly and gently slide the plate on to the centre of the place setting in front of the customer.

> **▶ ▶ ▶ TO DO**
>
> Write down the rules on which side you should serve customers from in your workplace (or base this activity on your favourite table service restaurant). Note when you might have to make an exception (for example, because you cannot get behind customers sitting in a corner scat).

Silver serving food

- Hold the service dish on the palm of the left hand (reverse if you are left handed), cushioned with a serving cloth.
- Present each dish to the customer(s) before starting to serve from it.
- A clean service spoon and fork should be used for each item.
  Large or delicate items may be served with two fish knives.
- Take the serving spoon and fork in the right hand (reverse if you are left handed).
- Bring the dish to the level of the customer's plate, just over the rim.
- Carefully lift the food with the spoon, using the fork to keep the item balanced and place on the plate in front of the customer.
- Tilt the dish slightly so that any sauce or gravy collects and can be served.
- Where a fish, for example, is too large for easy service, even by using two forks or knives splayed out, sever it across the middle with the spoon. Reassemble on the customer's plate.
- The appearance of the plate after serving should be attractive and appetising.

Using a serving spoon and fork

The curve of the fork should lie in the bowl of the spoon.

Hold the two together so that the palm of the hand and all the fingers are over both handles.

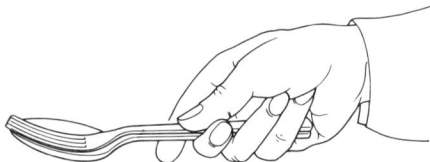

Make sure that the two are comfortably balanced.

Insert the first finger midway between the spoon and fork handles; this acts as a lever so that the fork prongs and spoon bowl may be opened and closed to hold the items securely.

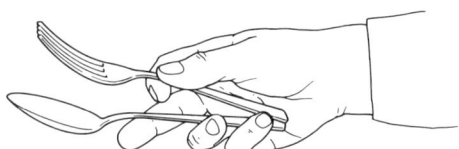

¶¶ SERVICE TIPS

Certain foods may be served using two service forks or two fish knives, for example omelettes, but this depends on the equipment available and the policy of the restaurant.

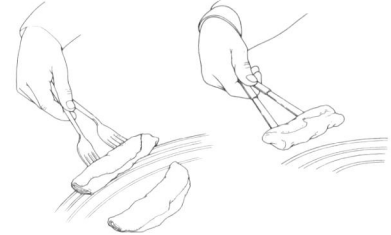

It may be easier to use the fork, prongs downwards, for example, when serving stuffed tomatoes.

When serving dishes with a pastry crust, the crust should be portioned and placed to one side, the filling spooned on to the plate and the crust placed on top of the filling.

Speed is an essential part of the silver service skill; there may be as many as ten portions of food on the 'flat', so ten customers have to be served before the food becomes cold. To achieve this, the food must be extremely hot when it leaves the kitchen.

▶ ▶ ▶ TO DO

If you are not yet skilled at using a spoon and fork to lift food, practise picking up:

- a medium-sized raw potato
- a slice of cold meat
- a slice of apple pie
- some Brussels sprouts
- or your own selection of different sized items.

Carrying plated food

For efficiency and speed, serving staff may need to carry three plated meals at once.

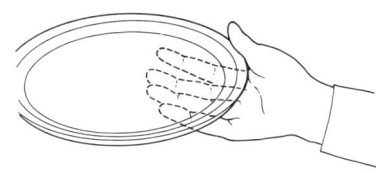

1. Pick up a plate with the right hand.
2. Hold out the first two fingers of the left hand making a platform with the third and fourth fingers.
3. Transfer the plate to the left hand placing it on the first two fingers and holding it firmly in position with the thumb.
4. Pick up a second plate with the right hand.
5. Place the second plate on the platform of the left hand.

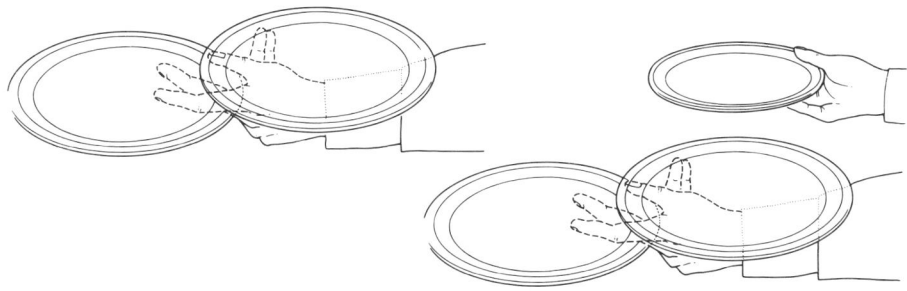

6. Make sure the two plates are balanced carefully, pick up a third plate in the right hand.

If you find it easier, use your left hand instead of the right (and vice versa) for these operations.

✱ FOR INTEREST

It is possible with practice to carry three plates in the left hand. Only the fourth finger is used to make the platform. The first plate is held between the thumb and first finger. The second plate is held between the first finger and second and third fingers. The third plate rests on the base of the thumb, wrist and tip of the fourth finger. The fourth plate is held in the right hand.

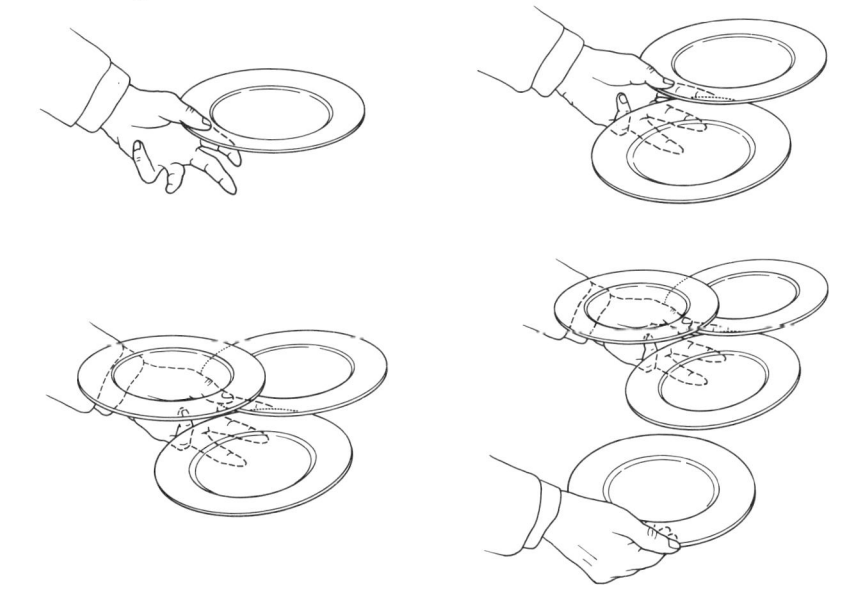

The information in units 7 to 10 will help you gain certification in the Caterbase modules *Serving and Clearing Food in Silver Service*, *Serving and Clearing Food in Plated Service* and *Serving and Clearing Food in Family Service*.

Plating food at a side table

1. Wheel the side table or trolley to the customers' table, positioning it so that there is less risk of getting in the way of other serving staff, and so that the customers can see the food service.
2. Assemble serving equipment (enough sets of spoons and forks etc. to be able to use clean utensils for each dish).
3. Bring the plates—hot for hot dishes, cold for cold dishes.
4. As soon as the food and the customers are ready to be served, bring the food from the kitchen and after presenting it to the customers, place the serving dish or flat on the side table.
5. Working as quickly as possible, transfer the portions of food to the customers' plates. As soon as each plate is ready, with any accompaning garnish, pick it up by the rim and take it to the customer, placing it down from the appropriate side.

6. Serving food in this way means that both hands are free and should be used to transfer the food from the serving dish to the customer's plate: for example, the spoon in the right hand, fork in the left.

Guéridon service

Elaborate preparation, such as filleting of cooked fish, carving poultry and game, cooking steaks, making sauces and finishing such dishes as pancakes, may be performed from a trolley, in front of the customer. A hot plate may be used to keep the food hot, or when cooking is carried out on the trolley, a gas or spirit lamp (réchaud) may be used.

Serving from a trolley

Food dishes may be displayed on a trolley in the dining area, and wheeled to the customers' table where they can make a selection from a choice of dishes that they can see.

Ideally all food on display should be covered and where food items are highly perishable, the displays should be kept chilled on a bed of crushed ice.

The trolley is arranged just before service commences, displaying sufficient dishes for customers to have a choice, without overloading. Plates and dishes are stacked on the lower shelf with sufficient serving spoons and forks. Clean serving utensils should be used for each food item. As one individual dish becomes empty or almost empty, it should be replaced by another to ensure a continuous selection of items.

The trolley is wheeled to the customers' table and placed next to the person to be served:

- An explanation is given (if required) of the dishes presented on the trolley.
- The appropriate plate is taken from the trolley or, in the case of hors d'oeuvres may be removed from the customer's place setting.
- The selected food items are placed on the plate, using a clean serving utensil for each item.
- The plate is placed in front of the customer.
- The trolley is wheeled to the side of the next customer to be served.

Types of food trolleys

1. **Hors d'oeuvres trolley** Assorted hors d'oeuvres are placed in dishes arranged on the top or placed on revolving shelves.
2. **Sweet trolley** The shelves are designed to enable sweets, such as gâteaux, trifle, mousses and fresh fruit salad, to be attractively displayed.
3. **Cheese trolley** This is usually a trolley with a roll top plastic lid, displaying a variety of cheeses, which may be decorated with a selection of fresh salad items and fruit.

Serving cheese from a board

1. Present the cheeseboard to the customer. The serving staff should know the names, types and flavours of the different cheeses.
2. A clean knife should be used to serve each cheese, especially blue and soft cheeses.
3. When the customer has made a selection, cut a neat portion and using the prong of the cheese knife, place the cheese on the customer's plate.
4. The biscuits may be offered to the customer or placed on the table.
5. If a customer requests some of the salad items, such as grapes, radishes or pickled onions, these should be placed on the plate with the cheese.

Equipment required for serving cheese

- side plate
- side knife
- sweet fork (optional)
- fresh dish of butter
- salt and pepper set
- basket of cheese biscuits
- grapes, celery and other fruit and salad items may also be served.

  TO DO

Visit a supermarket or shop with a good cheese selection. Make a list of the different cheeses that might be found on a cheeseboard. Choose from your list the cheeses that would make a good selection to offer to customers in a restaurant:

- specialising in French food
- offering only English food
- offering an inexpensive fixed price menu.

Try and choose at least six for each example (if possible, not duplicating your choice).

Important points to note when serving

1. The plates must be at the correct temperature; *hot* food must be served on *hot* plates and *cold* food on *cold* plates.
2. Serving staff should take care to hold hot plates with a cloth and warn customers not to touch very hot plates.
3. Cold dishes should be served before hot ones.
4. Where possible, serve female customers first, and the host last.
5. Do not touch the food on the plates.
6. Take care not to spill sauce or gravy on to the table when placing the plate down in front of the customer.
7. Make sure the plate rim is clean and has not been splashed; if this has happened, wipe it with a clean serving cloth.
8. In some restaurants, liner plates (plates used under the food plate) may be used when serving soup or dessert.
9. In many small restaurants, some accompaniments are the responsibility of the serving staff to prepare and offer to customers, for example:

   - English mustard (unless it is bought in ready made)
   - fresh hot toast (unless Melba toast is served)
   - buttered brown bread.

In larger establishments, such accompaniments may be made by staff in one of the ancillary departments (such as the still room), when it will be the responsibility of the serving staff to remember to collect them.

Other accompaniments which serving staff must remember to collect (either from their sideboard or the preparation area for the dining room) and offer to customers include:

- French mustard
- bought-in/proprietary sauces, such as tartare sauce and mayonnaise
- fresh cream.

Many accompaniments will be prepared by the chefs in the kitchen and these are collected at the same time as the dish. It is important to be familiar with what these are, so that in busy kitchens they are not overlooked in the belief they are for some other dish; examples are:

- gravy
- hollandaise sauce.

Presenting the dish to customers

When the food comes to the restaurant in a service dish, it should be presented to the customers before any is served. If the dish is to be silver served to one customer only, there is no need to present it as a separate step. However if the dish or flat holds several portions, the presentation allows all the customers to admire the dish in its entirety and indeed to confirm it is the one ordered. If there is a cover on the dish, this should be lifted carefully so that condensation is caught in the lid and does not drip on to the tablecloth or food. If a deep serving dish is used, it should be placed on a liner plate.

Some accompaniments

Dish	Accompaniment	Service
Starters		
Smoked fish, seafood, prawns, hors d'oeuvres	Brown bread, thinly sliced, buttered, crusts removed (optional), cut into triangles	Arranged on doyley-covered plate: • included on starter plate • offered to customer • placed on table • silver served
Pâtés and savoury mousses, such as ham	Hot, fresh toast, cut into triangles or fingers or Melba toast (thin dry toast)	Arranged in folded napkin or toast rack on plate: • placed on table

Fresh grapefruit or melon	Caster sugar and, for the melon, ground ginger	In bowls (sugar can be in shaker): • placed on table • offered to customer
Minestrone soup, French onion soup, some clear soups, pasta dishes	Parmesan cheese (grated finely)	In bowl or sauceboat: • offered to customer • grated over the dish in front of customer (with special grater)
Hors d'oeuvres, salads	Oil and vinegar *or* vinaigrette *or* mayonnaise	In glass bottles • placed on table In sauceboats • offered to customer • silver served
Purée soups and cream of tomato soup	Croûtons (small cubes of fried bread)	In sauceboat or bowl: • offered to customer • silver served
Fish dishes Fried fish	Wedge or half a lemon *and* tartare sauce *or* flavoured butter (such as parsley or anchovy)	On plate/service dish In sauceboat: • offered to customer • silver served On each portion In sauceboat (with iced water): • silver served
Grilled fish	As fried Hollandaise or similar sauce	In sauceboat: • silver served
Poached fish	Sauce made from cooking liquid	On each portion In sauceboat: • silver served
Roast meats All varieties	Gravy	On plate/service dish In sauceboat: • silver served
Lamb	Mint sauce	
Beef	Horseradish sauce	In sauceboat:
Pork	Apple sauce	• silver served
Chicken	Bread sauce	
Turkey	Cranberry sauce	
Other meat dishes Boiled leg of mutton	Caper sauce	In sauceboat: • silver served
Curry	Chutney	In sauceboat or proprietary jar: • placed on table • silver served
	Poppadums	In dish or basket: • offered to customer • silver served
	Coconut, various fruits	In dishes: • offered to customer • placed on table • silver served
Sweets Sponges Hot sponges, pies, puddings	Custard	In sauceboat: • offered to customer • silver served
Cold pies, pastries, gâteaux, fruit salad	Cream	In sauceboat/jug: • offered to customer • silver served • placed on table As part of garnish
Ice cream	Wafer biscuits, various sweet sauces, such as raspberry, hot chocolate	With dish In sauceboat: • silver served

19

Clearing after courses

In general

- Clear the sideboard, if used.
- Put away or return to the kitchen/service area any unused equipment.
- Collect any cold accompaniments for the next course.
- Wait until all the customers have finished eating before starting to clear the table.
- Remove any clean plates, cutlery and glasses that will not be required in later courses, using a service plate.

After the main course

- In some restaurants, the cruet set (salt and pepper) and butter dish are removed from the customers' table just before they finish eating, in others these items are left until the main course is cleared.
- Use a neatly folded napkin as a brush (unless the restaurant has a special brush crumb remover) to bring any crumbs and broken pieces of bread to the edge of the table. From the edge of the table they can be brought gently on to a medium-sized plate, and removed from the dining area.

If a sweet is to be served:

- Place a sweet spoon on the right and sweet fork on the left of the place setting (or move them down from the top of the setting).
- See unit 8 for service of sweets and cheese from a trolley, and serving from a cheeseboard.

How to clear plates

- Removing first plate
1. Approach the customer from the appropriate side, see unit 6.
2. Leaning forward slightly, take a firm hold of the plate with the thumb over the rim and the first two fingers under it.
3. Remove the plate from the customer, moving back away from the customer as you do so.
4. Transfer the plate to the other hand, taking hold of it with the thumb on top of the rim and the first two fingers stretched out on the underside. The third and fourth fingers should be crooked upwards ready to receive the second plate.

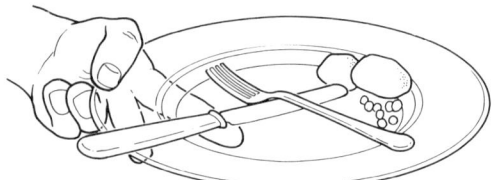

5. With the free hand, gently scrape any remaining food into a pile with a fork.
6. Arrange the knife and fork at right angles, with the knife blade under the bridge of the fork.

- Second plate stage
7. Remove the second customer's plate.
8. Transfer it to the other hand, resting it on the platform you have formed with the tips of the third and fourth fingers, the base of the thumb and the lower part of the forearm.
9. Remove the knife from this plate and slip it under the fork on the first plate. Ensure this second plate is level and safely balanced.
10. Using the second fork, carefully scrape any remaining food off, on to the first plate. This should be carried out standing well away from the customers. The debris should be piled on to the first plate so that items are not going to roll off.

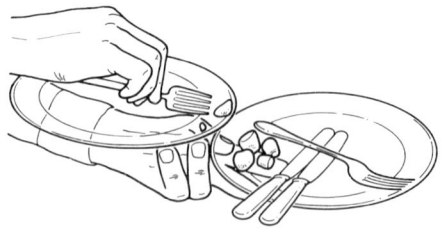

❚❚ SERVICE TIP

When to clear?   Clearing should commence when all the customers at the table have finished eating. At a function the head waiter usually gives a signal for clearing to start. When the host of the party is known, this should be the last plate cleared from the table. Clearing should be carried out systematically around the table, in such a way that none of the customers feels forgotten.

11. Place the second fork with the first on the lower plate.
12. Continue to clear plates until the table is cleared, or no more plates can be carried safely (eight is normally the maximum).

   ● Completing clearing

13. A neat, secure stack of plates should be resting on the forearm, thumb and fingers.
14. Transfer the lower plate with the cutlery and debris to the top of the pile of plates.
15. Take the pile of plates to the sideboard or directly to the wash-up area.

Clearing soup dishes   The plate clearing procedure has to be adapted when soup dishes with their liner plates are to be cleared.

● After the second dish has been removed, the liner plate is kept on the platform formed by the tips of the third and fourth fingers, the base of the thumb and the lower part of the forearm.
● The soup spoon from the first (lower) is transferred to the second (upper) dish.
● The second (upper) dish and the spoons are then transferred to the lower plate. The liner plate is kept at the upper level if more dishes and plates are to be cleared.

● For subsequent dishes and plates, the procedure is repeated:
   ● liner and dish placed on the upper liner plate(s)
   ● spoons transferred to the upper dish (the one most recently cleared)
   ● upper dish and spoons transferred to lower pile
   ● liner plate remains in the upper pile.
● When clearing is complete, the lower pile including the base liner is placed on top of the pile of liners at the upper level.
● The pile is then carried to the sideboard or directly to the washing up area, having been slipped down off the platform formed by the fingers, thumb and forearm to the palm of the hand and the second hand used to take half the weight.

🍴 **SERVICE TIPS**

● The right or left hand?
Plates are normally removed with the right hand and then transferred to the left for stacking. If left handed, it may be preferable to use the left hand for removing the plate and the right for stacking.
● Which way up should the forks be placed?
It may be the practice of the restaurant to place forks, prongs downwards on the lower plate to form a larger bridge under which to place the knife blades.
● How can food or cutlery be prevented from falling off?
Cutlery can be prevented from sliding around the stacking plate by positioning the first fork so that the thumb can hold it against the plate. Knives and forks should be angled so that if any fall off the plate, it will not be in the customer's direction.
● Dealing with a lot of debris
When there is a lot of debris left on the plates, it may be easier to clear a few plates at a time, and remove to the sideboard or the wash-up area.
● Noise
Clearing should be carried out as quietly as possible. Handle the cutlery gently but firmly, do not bang the plates when scraping or piling them.
● Clearing rapidly
Once a bit of experience has been gained, the process can be carried out more quickly by:
   ● transferring cutlery and any debris to the lower plate, as the server moves from one customer to the next
   ● once clearing is completed, transferring the lower plate to the top of the pile, while removing to the sideboard.
● Alternative methods
Occasionally a silver tray may be used to clear tables. The tray is held in one hand and the pile of plates built on this. In stately homes, the custom is to clear one plate at a time, stacking the plates on the sideboard.

Using a tray

It can be easier, quicker and safer to carry plates, food dishes and other items for service on a tray, rather than carrying stacks of plates in the hands and making frequent trips back and forwards between the dining area and the kitchen.

On most occasions, however, trays should not be taken to the table to clear used plates, or to bring food, while the customers are seated. The tray should be placed on a side table, from where serving and clearing can be carried out. Exceptions are fast food restaurants where trays aid fast clearing.

How to lift a loaded tray

1. Take hold of the right edge (reverse if you are left handed) about half way along.
2. Bending forward, position the left forearm (reverse if you are left handed) with fingers spread wide, in a position about mid way along the length of the tray, and at the same height as the surface on which it is resting.
3. Carefully pull the tray with the right hand on to the left forearm.
4. The left hand should be positioned, palm upwards, under the heaviest part of the tray.

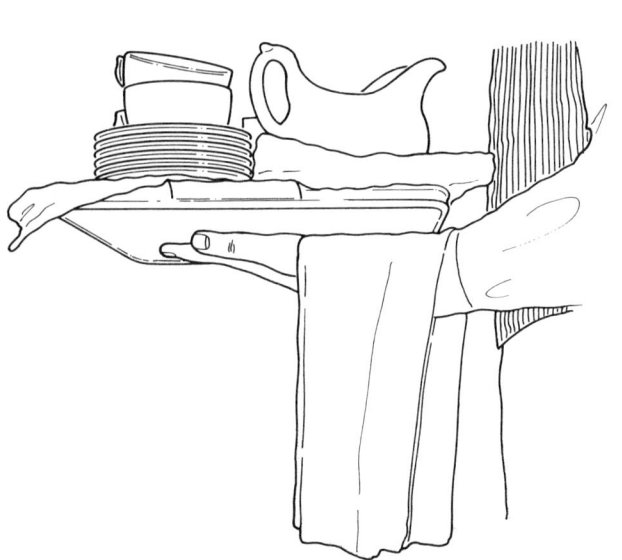

5. Lift the tray either to waist height or to shoulder height. Make sure it is well balanced and level.

Points to note when carrying trays

- Trays should be carefully balanced on one arm so that the other is free to open doors or to place drinks on the table.
- A clean napkin should be placed on the tray to prevent items from slipping.
- Do not carry bottles of wine or mineral water on a tray, except when using cradlers or wine coolers. Split-size (individual) mineral bottles are sometimes carried.
- Do not overload the tray, it must be possible to carry it.
- Make sure it is securely stacked.
- Place the heaviest article in the middle with lighter items around it, this aids balance.
- Take care when removing an item from a tray, that it is still balanced.
- Teapot and sauceboat spouts should be positioned to point away from the carrier, to avoid burns from accidental spills.
- Glasses should not be carried on the same tray as dishes, the glasses may crack as the tray is moved.

Carrying glassware

When handling glassware in front of customers a tray should always be used.

When laying glassware on the table before service commences, the serving staff may carry the glasses in the hand.

How to carry clean wine goblets

- Spread the fingers of the left hand, palm upwards. Pick up a glass by the stem and place it upside down with the base resting on the middle two fingers.
- Place a second glass between the first and second fingers, wedging the base under the base of the first glass.
- Place a third glass between the third and fourth fingers, again with the base wedged firmly under the base of the first glass.

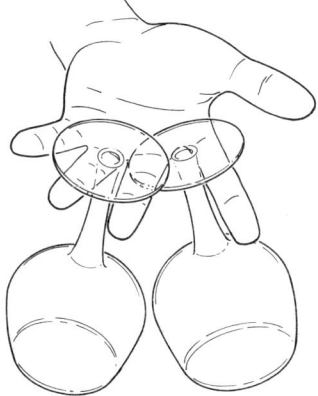

- Place a fourth glass between the thumb and first finger with the base wedged under the base of the second glass.
- All glasses should be pushed back well between the fingers to allow further glasses to be inserted in the same order.
- When putting glasses down, remove them in the reverse order.

SERVICE TIPS

Handling glasses   Glasses should be transferred from the tray to the table or vice versa by picking them up individually, by the stem or handle, or firmly grasping the outside.

Fingers should never be placed inside the glasses.

  TO DO

Serving staff handle plates, cutlery and glasses throughout the serving procedures. Make a list of the stages when these items are handled in your workplace (or a restaurant of your choice). Against each entry on your list note any special handling techniques, including when a tray is used. Tick those techniques you are well practised in using, and put a star by those you need further practice to do proficiently. Try and practise these at home.

Serving staff may be called upon to serve non-alcoholic beverages, for example tea and coffee, in a variety of locations at any time of the day or night.

The beverage may be ordered:

- on its own
- with a meal or snack
- after a meal.

The way in which the beverage is served will depend on the type of drink, the style of the restaurant and the time of day. It may be:

1. Ready poured into a cup.
2. Poured from a central pot at the customers' table by the serving staff.
3. Placed on the table in a pot for customers to serve themselves.
4. Served from a tray at the customers' table by the serving staff.

Procedure for serving tea at the table   The serving staff bring to the table, on a tray:

- a pot of tea, of a suitable size
- a pot of hot water (for customers to alter the strength of the tea)
- cold milk and/or lemon slices
- white sugar, loose, cubed or in sachets (this may already be on the table)
- a tea strainer and a bowl for slops (unless a tea bag is used to make the tea)
- cups, saucers and teaspoons (unless they are already on the table).

The tea and hot water pots are placed on the table, usually on to plates or stands. The handles should be facing the customer who is going to pour the tea.

When tea is served in a pot, it is always served by the customer.

Teas

Various kinds of 'Teas' are offered in restaurants, from a cup of tea and a piece of cake to a full 'High Tea', in effect a meal of two courses. Items may be priced individually, or a set price charged for the tea menu.

1. Afternoon tea   A selection of tea blends may be served, for example Assam, Earl Grey, China.

Toasted items should be brought to the table as soon as possible, and left for customers to serve themselves.

In some restaurants, the side plates and knives used for savoury items (such as sandwiches, toast etc.) are replaced with clean before the service of cakes and pastries.

Gâteaux and cakes may be arranged on a plate and placed on the table or the customers may make a choice from a selection on a sweet trolley.

2. High tea   Tea is usually served, but coffee, chocolate, milk and fruit drinks may also be offered.

The place setting is normally the same as for breakfast (see unit 15).

3. Buffet teas   Buffet teas may be served when there are a large number of customers requiring service at the same time, such as at a wedding reception.

The buffet table is laid out in advance with teacups, saucers and spoons, plates and knives, milk jugs and sugar bowls. Just before service starts, the food items are placed on the table and the tea is prepared.

The tea may be poured to order by the serving staff, it may be pre-poured or it may be left for the customers to help themselves.

The information in units 12 and 13 will help you gain the Caterbase module *Serving and Clearing of Beverages in Restaurant Service.*

● Equipment needed for afternoon tea

1. Teacup, saucer, teaspoon
2. Side plate with side knife and pastry fork
3. Napkin
4. Slop basin and tea strainer
5. Sugar basin with tongs for lump sugar, spoon for loose
6. Underplates for tea/hot water jugs
7. Cold milk jug
8. Preserve dishes with teaspoons
9. Butter dish
10. Cream dish.

▶ ▶ ▶ TO DO

Make a list of the steps to follow when preparing and serving afternoon tea for small parties of customers in a situation of your choice (such as a hotel lounge or cafe). If possible, ask someone who has never served tea to carry out the task for two customers, by following your instructions. Note any steps which you do not appear to have explained well or have forgotten.

Coffee

Coffee may be ordered at any time of the day or night, but the most common times to serve coffee are mid-morning and after a meal.

1. Morning coffee   Morning coffee may be served in:

- hotel lounges
- conference and meetings rooms
- bistros and coffee shops
- department store restaurants.

Although coffee is usually served, several other hot or cold beverages may be offered as alternatives, such as tea, chocolate or milk. Sweet biscuits or a selection of pastries are often served with the beverage.

- Hotel lounges
  The serving staff in the lounge take the order from the customers, and assemble the necessary items on a small tray. This is then taken to the table, where the items are unloaded. The first cup may be poured by the serving staff or the customers may serve themselves.
- Conference and meeting rooms
  Morning coffee may be served in the room while a meeting is in progress, or there may be a break for coffee, which may then be served outside the room.

Service will vary according to which method is used:

Inside the room   1. Cups of coffee are poured then carried into the room on trays, and distributed by the serving staff. Milk and sugar are placed on tables around the room for customers to help themselves.
2. At small meetings, the cups and saucers may be distributed around the table, then the coffee pot, milk and sugar placed on the table for the customers to help themselves.
3. Portable filter coffee machines may be installed in the meeting room on a side table. The serving staff will prepare jugs of coffee and leave them on the hot plate for customers to serve themselves. Milk, sugar and biscuits are left on the side. Items are replenished as necessary.

Outside the room   A service table is prepared outside the meeting room, with the required number of cups. Milk, sugar and biscuits are also laid out. Serving staff pour the coffee during the coffee break. Tea may also be provided.

2. Serving coffee after a meal   Customers may take coffee at the dining table once the rest of the meal has been cleared or they may take coffee in the lounge, where available. This may be more pleasant for the customer and more convenient for the serving staff, who can then prepare the table for the next sitting.

Serving coffee from a tray

1. Approach the customer from the side the cup is positioned, usually the right.

> ✱ **FOR INTEREST**
>
> - Coffee shops
> A range of different ground coffees may be available. Hot milk or cream, and brown sugar is provided. Speciality coffees, such as cappuccino or expresso, may also be served. Pastries, biscuits and cakes are served with the coffee.

2. Enquire if the customer would like sugar. Place the required number of spoonfuls in the cup.

3. Rotate the tray on the flat of the palm so that the spout of the coffee pot is pointing towards the customer's cup with the handles towards the server.
4. Enquire if milk or cream is required.
5. If the customer wants milk or cream, pour the coffee until the cup is two-thirds full.

6. Rotate the tray until the milk spout is above the cup, pivot the jug to add milk or cream to the coffee.
7. Be careful not to fill the cup too full, ½ cm (¼ inch) from the top of the cup is sufficient.
8. If coffee spills into the saucer while serving, apologise to the customer, remove the cup and saucer, replace it with a clean set and re-serve the coffee.
9. If the coffee service is interrupted for any reason, make sure that the coffee in the pot has not gone cold, when service is resumed.

Serving coffee without a tray

Coffee may be served from a central pot, which when not in use is kept on a hot plate on the side.

- Place the milk or cream and sugar on the table for customers to help themselves.
- Hold the coffee pot in the right hand.
- In some restaurants a service cloth is wrapped around the pot and twisted around the handle. This keeps the coffee hot, protects hands from heat, and catches drips from the spout.
- If hot milk is being offered, it may also be kept on the hot plate. In this case it is offered at the same time as the coffee (the jug is held in the left hand).

When serving coffee after lunch or dinner a smaller cup, called a demi-tasse, may be used. It holds half the quantity of a tea cup.

 SERVICE TIP

Before pouring the coffee:

1. Check that a clean cup, saucer and spoon of the correct size are in place on the table.
2. The cup should not be placed directly in front of the customer but slightly to one side (the side from which the beverage will be served). The handle of the cup should be pointing to the right of the customer (so that it can be easily lifted up) with the coffee spoon lying under it, handle also towards the customer.
3. Once the coffee has been poured, the cup is moved to a position directly in front of the customer.

▶ ▶ ▶ TO DO

Visit a specialist coffee shop or a supermarket with a good range of coffee. Note the different varieties, find out as much as you can about them and the different ways coffee can be made. Find a suitable blend that could be served where you work; suggest the best way in which to make it.

In large restaurants a wine waiter may serve any alcoholic beverages including aperitifs, wine and liqueurs. The wine waiter or 'sommelier' may also be required to serve tobacco and cigars, and ensure that these items are paid for. In many restaurants, however, the food service staff are required to serve the wine and other drinks.

1. Presenting the wine list

- Offer the wine list to the customers after the food order has been taken.
- Present the wine list open. Do not leave the table immediately, the customers may need advice with the order.

It is important to know:

- if the wine is red, white or rosé
- if the wine is still, sparkling, or semi-sparkling
- if the wine is dry, medium or sweet
- which wines improve the taste of which foods.

2. Take the wine order

Record: the date
table number
the name or number of the wine
the number of bottles or glasses required.

3. Preparing for service   The serving staff will need:

- the appropriate wine glasses, clean, polished and not chipped or cracked
- a wine bucket to keep white/rosé wines chilled
- a wine basket or side plate for red wine
- a corkscrew
- a clean service cloth
- the bottle of wine.

4. Serving the wine

- Present the chosen wine to the customer with the label clearly displayed.
- Cut through the foil around the top of the neck and remove. Leave the rest of the foil in place. In this way the wine does not come into contact with the foil when it is being poured, but the top of the bottle still looks attractive.
- Wipe the top of the neck and cork with a clean dry cloth.
- Insert a corkscrew into the centre of the cork, turning the corkscrew and not the bottle.
- Gently and cleanly pull out the cork. Do not shake the bottle in the process.
- Wipe clean the mouth of the bottle.
- The wine is ready to be poured.

5. Pouring the wine   Pour a little wine into the glass of the customer who gave the order, for sampling.

When approved, continue serving the wine. Serve in a clockwise direction, female customers first, then the male customers, ending with the person who made the order.

🍴 SERVICE TIP

Wine is drunk to complement food, so customers will wish to order the wine when they have decided on the food they are going to eat.

A popular corkscrew among serving staff is one which incorporates a blade and a lever—the so-called 'waiter's friend'

✳ FOR INTEREST

Many restaurants do not use wine buckets or baskets, the wine is simply placed on the table.

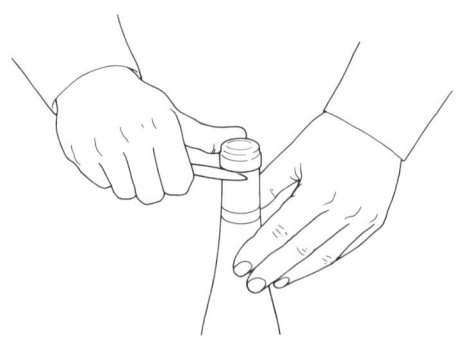

Hold the bottle, label uppermost so that it can be read, with the hand over it, thumb round one side, fingers around the other and the index finger lying up the shoulder.

Place the lip of the bottle just over the edge of the glass and tip the bottle downwards until the wine begins to flow. Do not let the bottle touch the rim of the glass.

Having poured each glass ½ to ⅔rds full, twist the bottle gently to prevent any drips from falling on the table, and remove the drips from the bottle with the cloth.

Leave the bottle either in the basket or bucket or on the table for customers to serve themselves.

The serving staff should top up the glasses regularly.

Note: when serving a second bottle of wine, clean glasses should be provided, even if it is the same wine.

6. Opening sparkling wine   Sparkling wine is kept slightly colder than white wine; it should not be shaken.

Sparkling wines have a different type of seal, a shaped cork held in place with wire covered in foil.

- The wine is presented in the same way as still wines.
- Point the neck of the bottle into a corner of the room, remove the foil.
- Slowly untwist the wire and loosen it around the cork.
- Hold the neck of the bottle with one hand and the cork with the other; the cork should give a very gentle pop and be removed easily.
- The wine should then be poured without delay (otherwise it may froth up out of the bottle).
- Place the bottle in a wine cooler, next to the table.

Serving temperature of wine

Red wine	room temperature	18°C	(65°F)
Dry white and rosé	cooled	10°C	(50°F)
Sweet white and sparkling	chilled	7 to 8°C	(45 to 47°F)

Other alcoholic beverages

1. Aperitifs   Customers may order aperitifs before the meal. Carefully chosen they act as appetisers, stimulating the palate. These are often drunk in the bar, before entering the restaurant. When a restaurant does not have a bar, the aperitifs are consumed at the table.

The service of aperitifs should be carried out as quickly as possible so that the customers can enjoy the drink while they are choosing and ordering their meal.

2. Liqueurs   These are usually served after the meal. Liqueur glasses vary according to the preference of the restaurant. In most high class restaurants the liqueur bottle is taken to the table and presented to the customers, the glasses being poured in front of them.

Serving other drinks

- Carry the drinks on a cloth covered salver or tray.
- Place the drinks down on the right hand side of the customer.
- If a mixer has been ordered, pour the required amount into the glass and leave the bottle with the remainder on the table.
- If a second round of drinks is ordered, always serve them in fresh glasses.

✱ FOR INTEREST

Before serving wine it is sometimes usual to smell the cork. If any unpleasant odour is detected, this would indicate that the cork has gone musty and the mustiness has been absorbed by the wine. However some experts say it is impossible to detect a bad wine in this way.

✱ FOR INTEREST

Wine bottles with an indent in the base, such as champagne, may be poured with the hand holding the base; however care should be taken as the grip will not be as firm as the more standard way of holding.

Examples of aperitifs

Sherry   Generally classified as 'dry', 'medium' or 'sweet'.
Aperitif wines   Including Dubonnet, Madeira and vermouth.
Spirits   Whisky, gin and vodka may be ordered as an aperitif.
Cocktails   There are hundreds of different cocktail mixes.

◆ ◆ ◆ TO DO

Collect several examples of wine labels; record next to each label, the colour of the wine, whether still or sparkling, sweet or dry and what foods it might complement.

The information in this unit will help you gain the Caterbase modules in *Table Service of Wine* and *Table Service of Alcoholic Beverages*.

- Breakfast is generally eaten as the first meal of the day. It is often the last meal eaten by a hotel guest and the way in which it is served will contribute to the customer's final impression of the establishment and its staff.
- Customers are likely to expect very punctual service at breakfast; they may be prepared to wait to be served at lunchtime but first thing in the morning a wait of more than a few minutes may be unacceptable.
- The breakfast meal may vary in size from a cup of coffee and a croissant to a substantial meal of several courses.

✳ FOR INTEREST

Breakfast meals served at midday are called *brunch*.

All the items that might comprise a typical English breakfast

Preparing the dining room for service

Some of the dining room preparations can be made the previous night, such as laying cloths, cutlery and crockery. Tables require a lot of preparation as more items are set on them than at any other meal. By carrying out some of the preparatory procedures the night before, serving staff can ensure that all is ready for service in the morning. All equipment laid out the night before should be covered with a clean cloth.

Morning preparation

1. Sugar (lump and soft), milk, preserves (jam and marmalade etc.) and mustard are placed on the tables.
2. Butter is prepared on plates and kept cool until required.
3. Fruit juices are poured into jugs.
4. Bowls of stewed and fresh fruit are prepared.
5. Grapefruit halves are collected, ready cut, from the kitchen.
6. If iced water is to be offered to customers on arrival, this must be prepared.

The fruit juices and stewed fruit may be kept chilled, on a bed of crushed ice or in a chilled cabinet, alongside cereals and other cold items on the buffet table for customers to help themselves.

✳ FOR INTEREST

Breakfast may be served on a tray in a hotel room. It is more common for Continental style breakfasts to be ordered in this way, as English breakfasts require more cutlery and crockery and are more difficult to keep hot.

All the hot items, for example, porridge and warm toast, are collected as required from the kitchen.

Some establishments prefer staff to collect each item, hot or cold, as it is ordered from the kitchen.

Buffet service

Many restaurants now offer a buffet breakfast service in preference to full table service:

- it is quicker
- it allows more freedom for customers
- it is economical on staff.

The buffet table may be prepared with a clean table cloth, crockery, cutlery and glasses the night before. The food is placed on the table just before the start of breakfast service.

The customers serve themselves to starters, returning to the buffet table again to select the main course. Sometimes starters are placed on the buffet table and the main course items are brought to the tables by the serving staff.

Service staff will still need to clear plates and equipment from the tables while breakfast service is commencing. They will also need to serve beverages.

What is served for breakfast?

Breakfast is a meal that differs widely throughout the world; it may include cheese, eggs, cold cooked meats, hot meats, smoked fish, chocolate and salads.

The two most common types of breakfast menus to be found are:

English breakfast A traditional breakfast can consist of as many as five courses, including:

- Stewed fruit and/or fruit juice
- Cold cereal or hot porridge
- Fish—fried, grilled or kedgeree
- Eggs—fried, boiled, poached, scrambled or omelette
- Meat—for example fried or grilled bacon and sausage with tomatoes and mushrooms (and, often, eggs)
- Fresh fruit
- Toast, bread and croissants
- Beverages—tea, coffee or chocolate.

Continental breakfast This usually consists of one or two courses with a beverage, for example:

- Fruit juice and/or fresh fruit
- Rolls, croissants, toast with butter, and preserves or honey
- Coffee, tea or chocolate.

Service of hot rolls and toast Bread rolls, croissants and brioches are normally left on the table at the start of service, for customers to help themselves from the basket.

Toast is brought from the kitchen as required, either in a toast rack or wrapped in a napkin in a basket or on a plate. It must be served *hot* and *fresh*.

Service of beverages The most common hot beverages requested at breakfast time are coffee and tea. Hot chocolate, hot milk and herbal teas may also be ordered. Some restaurants use the same sort of pots to serve coffee and tea, others keep different styles for each.

Examples of procedure for service

English breakfast

Take order for beverage, and fruit juice (in some restaurants).
Present menu.
Serve beverage.
Take order, noting any special requests (such as lightly boiled egg).
Adjust place settings.
Serve starter.
Serve rolls, and beverage if not already served.
Clear starter.
Serve main course.
Remove any unwanted items.
Clear main course.
Check table for butter and jam.
Serve more beverages and toast as required.

Continental breakfast

Present menu.
Take order.
Adjust place setting, if necessary.
Serve starter.
Serve hot beverage, check milk and sugar are on the table.
Serve hot rolls and/or toast.

‼ REMEMBER

When service is to take place at the table, the place settings will need adjusting after the order has been taken, spare cutlery should be removed and additional cutlery brought to the table.

Hot breakfast items are best suited to plated styles of service, as they are difficult to silver serve and do not keep well, becoming cold and unpresentable quickly.

Note should be taken of customers' cooking preferences, such as crispy bacon.

  TO DO

Make up a breakfast menu covering a choice of Continental and English breakfast items, to suit your workplace or a restaurant of your choice. What items could be placed on a buffet table for customers to help themselves?

A bill is a totalled list of charges relating to food and drinks consumed. The bill should be presented to the person who has been in charge of ordering the food and/or drinks at the end of the meal (see unit 9). If it is not certain to whom the bill should be presented, then it should be placed in the centre of the table.

Billing

The information included on a bill will vary between restaurants, but will include some of the following details:

Example of a typical bill

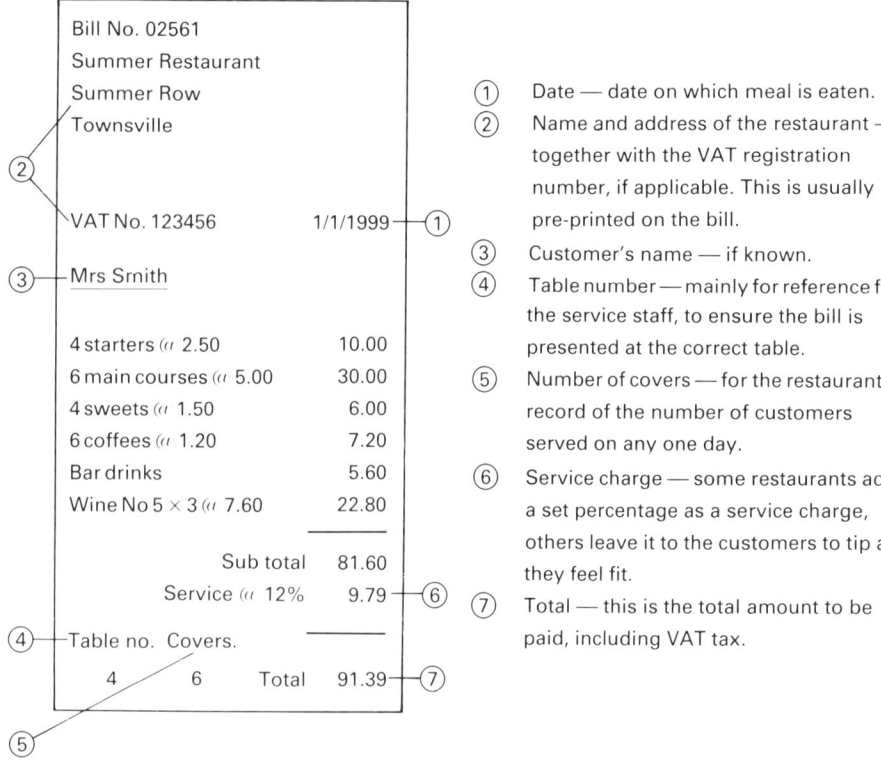

1. Date — date on which meal is eaten.
2. Name and address of the restaurant — together with the VAT registration number, if applicable. This is usually pre-printed on the bill.
3. Customer's name — if known.
4. Table number — mainly for reference for the service staff, to ensure the bill is presented at the correct table.
5. Number of covers — for the restaurant's record of the number of customers served on any one day.
6. Service charge — some restaurants add a set percentage as a service charge, others leave it to the customers to tip as they feel fit.
7. Total — this is the total amount to be paid, including VAT tax.

> ## USEFUL TERMS
>
> **VAT** Value Added Tax charged on many goods and services, paid to the government. Each restaurant with a large enough turnover has to register with the government and is given a special VAT registration number. Menu prices must be shown inclusive of VAT.
>
> **Service charge** An extra charge for service of a set percentage (usually between 5 and 15% and always stated clearly on the menu) which some restaurants add to the cost of customers' food and drinks. The total service charge which is collected forms part of the staff's wages (usually as an extra), and is divided according to the procedure of the restaurant.
>
> **Cover charge** A set amount per customer (how much must be stated clearly on the menu) which is added to the customers' bills.
>
> **Float** A sum of money (mostly coins, but possibly including some £5 notes) which is placed in the till at the start of service so that change can be given to customers. At the end of service the value of the float will be removed for safe keeping (and exchanged if necessary for more small change), leaving the takings.

Preparing the bill The method used to prepare the bill will vary; many restaurants now use a mechanical billing system, where all charges are entered into the machine, either directly by the serving staff or by a cashier, and the details are printed on the bill when required. In other circumstances the serving staff may be required to total the bill from the order checks.

Presenting the bill The bill should be presented either when the customer requests it or at the end of the meal after the coffee has been served. The bill is folded in half so that only the host knows the total charge and usually placed on a plate, small tray, or in a folder, and taken to the table. The serving staff should leave the customer to check the details and place the payment on the plate, returning to sort out any queries and to take the payment.

Taking payment

1. *Cash* Count the money carefully in front of the customer, take it to the till and return with the customer's copy of the bill and any change.
2. *Cheque* Make sure the cheque is filled out correctly, and that a valid cheque card is supporting the cheque. Amounts over £50 or in some cases £100 will require other identification, such as a current driving licence or a passport.

‼️ **REMEMBER**

Cheque checkpoints

Check the cheque:
- Is the *date* correct?
- Does the *amount* in words and figures agree?
- Does the signature match that on the card?
- Was the cheque signed in front of you?

Check the cheque card:
- Has the card expired?
- Does the signature match the one on the cheque?
- Does the code number match the one on the cheque?

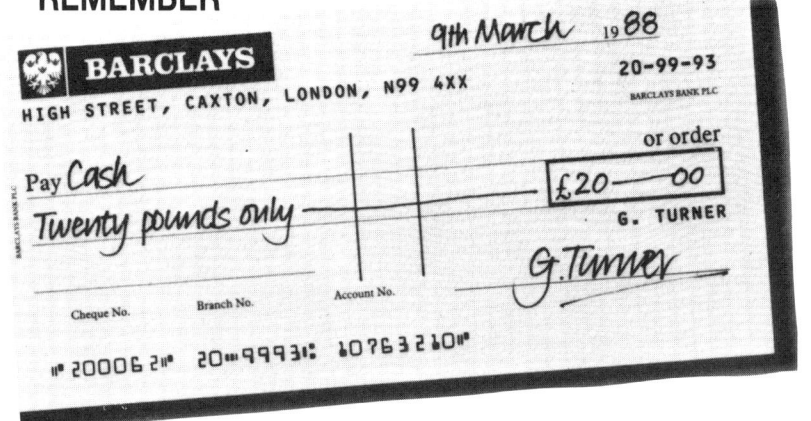

Write the cheque card number on the back of the cheque.

3. *Credit cards*   Many customers now pay by credit card, eg Access, Barclaycard, American Express.

- Check that the restaurant accepts the particular card.
- Check the details on the card carefully.
- Fill out a credit sales voucher.
- Present the voucher to the customer for signing.
- Put the voucher and the card through the imprinter/mechanised till.
- Give the appropriate copy of the voucher to the customer, with the credit card and receipt.
- Place the other copies in the appropriate place, usually in the till.

‼️ **REMEMBER**

Security   Security is important when handling cash, cheques or credit card vouchers.

Do not
- leave money lying around.
- leave the till unattended.
- leave the till drawer open.
- carry large amounts of money around.

Do
- check all figures carefully.
- hand over money as soon as possible.

‼️ **REMEMBER**

Credit card checkpoints

Check the card:
- Is the card accepted by the restaurant?
- Has the card expired?
- Is the card in the same name as the payee?
- Is the card on a list of lost or stolen cards?

Check the voucher:
- Is the *date* and *amount* filled in correctly?
- Has the information from the card been imprinted clearly?
- Does the customer's signature match the one on the card?

⮞ ⮞ ⮞ **TO DO**

Practise writing out a bill for food and drinks of your choice assuming you are entertaining three friends. Base the prices on a local restaurant menu. Check that VAT is included and what service charge should be added. Ask your tutor or supervisor to check your calculations.

4. *Account*   Regular customers may have an account at the restaurant. This means that they will not be asked to pay the bill at the time they have a meal or drink.

- Present the bill in the usual way.
- When the customer has checked and signed it, hand it to the cashier or place it in the till. Make sure the details of where the bill should be sent to are known (check with the cashier/manager).

The information in this unit will help you gain the Caterbase module *Billing and Taking Payment for Restaurant Service*.

Service has two distinct aspects:

- The various methods or procedures used in serving food to customers covered in units 4–16.
- Conviviality, the attitudes, behaviour and verbal skills that the serving staff display in their interaction with customers. The customer expects to be liked, to be respected, to feel important, relaxed and comfortable, while having a meal.

Attitudes, behaviour and verbal skills

The customers' perception of the quality of service will be influenced by the attitude of serving staff, their behaviour and what they say. Four skills are important:

1. Attentiveness This is the skill in observing or noticing what a customer wants and providing for that need: in other words, treating customers as people, not 'covers' or 'seats'.

Certain needs can be established from the type of customer, for example:

Children	may need extra napkins, small glasses, high chairs and, where possible, smaller portions.
Business entertainment customers	will expect attentive but unobtrusive service, that does not interfere with business discussions.
Groups	need special attention; a same-sex group is likely to require a more informal service and will be less inhibited than a mixed group.
Single customers	need to be treated with respect and tact (avoid a sneering greeting 'table for two?') and offered a table in a pleasant but quiet corner rather than in the centre of the room.
Special celebration customers	are looking for an occasion they will remember happily, so will be responsive to a show of serving skills at their most flamboyant, enjoying being seen celebrating (allow the champagne cork to make a discreet pop).

Dealing with drunkenness The serving staff should report any signs of drunkenness to the manager or supervisor, who will decide on whether to continue serving the customers or not. Serving staff should be tactful, quietly spoken, and not respond to any argument.

  TO DO

Make your own list of groups of customer and write down what needs they may have. Make a practice of observing how people behave in situations where they receive service (eg shops, hairdressers, not just restaurants) As you note different types of needs not on your list, add them to the list.

Other needs can be established by observing the customers' behaviour or body language and listening to what they say and how they say it:

Behaviour or body language	Customers may give non-verbal signs that they are impatient, such as folding their arms. Closed menus usually mean they are waiting to order. When customers are looking around, assume they are looking for the server.
Listening to what they say	When customers show knowledge of the food and beverage products, this should be respected. If a customer has difficulty with the language, show patience and understanding.
Listening to how they say it	Listening to the tone of voice of a customer can say a lot about whether the customer is pleased or annoyed, impatient or relaxed, shy or outgoing.

See: Customercraft book and video.

2. Empathy and rapport This is the skill of seeing things from the customer's point of view, understanding how the customer feels and then taking account of this in providing an appropriate style of service.

In helping customers to feel relaxed and comfortable, serving staff show they genuinely have their interest at heart. A lack of rapport shows in a member of staff who is condescending and pompous.

3. Using the right body language This is the skill of understanding the effect that certain expressions, body movements and appearance have on customers, and adopting them accordingly irrespective of mood or tiredness.

- The *facial expression* of the serving staff will tell the customer whether they are really friendly, or whether they are bored with the job.
- A *smile* will immediately create a friendly, welcoming atmosphere.
- *Eye contact* implies sincerity, interest and trustworthiness.
- Slouched posture or shuffling feet give a bad impression, a deliberate *upright posture* implies confidence and enthusiasm.
- *Grooming* is another way in which the serving staff can show their concern. Clean faces, hair, hands and clothes show that a server is bothered about appearances and therefore more likely to be bothered about the customer.

Conviviality and sales The restaurant depends on the sale of food and drink. The serving staff are in effect the sales people. Effective selling requires respect, tact, consideration and care for the customer. When customers eat they expect to receive their money's worth from products and service. The attitude and behaviour of the serving staff can greatly contribute to the latter.

4. Using the right words in the right way at the right time The ability to say, in the right way, the right thing at the right time is the essence of communication and very important in providing for the customer's needs. The following are vital in contributing to a pleasant experience:

- Servers' tone of voice, their speed and volume of talking.
- The words they use in handling a problem.
- Their use of customers' names or a respectful 'sir' or 'madam'.
- Information they give about the menu and the help they provide.

If there has been a complaint it is important to ensure that warm and friendly relations have been re-established before the customers leave the restaurant, and that they feel that they will be welcomed on a return visit.

Dealing with complaints Any complaint about the service or food should be dealt with immediately, with an apology. If the complaint is about an order of food, the serving staff should:

- Apologise to the customer.
- Remove the dish from the table.
- Offer the menu, asking if another serving of the same dish is required or an alternative.
- Write out a special check for the new order.
- Lay a fresh place setting.
- Collect and serve the new dish as soon as possible.
- Apologise for the inconvenience.
- Enquire if the new dish is satisfactory.
- The policy of the restaurant will dictate whether the customer is charged for the new dish or not.

Serving involves close contact with customers and food, and means that individual staff members are under constant close observation. It is therefore important for staff to maintain high standards of personal presentation, including personal hygiene and dress.

Personal hygiene

Service must always be carried out in a clean and hygienic way to protect customers against food poisoning and the spread of disease. Dirt and dirty practices makes eating food unsafe as well as unpleasant.

1. Fingernails and hands   These are always on show. It is vital to wash hands immediately before service and after using the toilet. Nails should be trimmed and kept clean. Although many establishments do not insist, it is preferable to avoid nail polish. Smokers should take special care that their hands are clean.

2. Bodily cleanliness   Any odour will be offensive to customers, frequent bathing is important. Scent and perfume should be avoided.

3. Clear complexion   A member of the serving staff who looks unhealthy will not do much to advertise the health standards of the restaurant. A clear skin and complexion depends to a large extent on having adequate sleep, exercise and a balanced diet. A healthy person will also be better able to carry out the duties of the job. Make-up should be used sparingly.

4. Hair   This should be kept clean and away from the face, and away from food.

5. Mouth   Clean teeth and breath are important as serving staff are often in close proximity to customers and do not want to cause offence.

6. Feet   Feet need care for comfort and hygiene. Toe nails should be trimmed frequently.

7. Ill health   When a member of staff has a cold or is feeling unwell, it is better for him or her to stay away from work, than to risk infecting other staff members or customers. Germs can be transmitted quickly when handling food.

Important points to remember:

- Never lick the fingers.
- Keep hands really clean.
- Never touch the hair.
- Protect cuts and grazes with a clean dressing.
- Avoid using a handkerchief in the restaurant.
- Do not eat, drink or chew while on duty.
- Do not smoke on duty.
- Never touch food on the plates.

Clothing

Whether a uniform is provided by the restaurant or serving staff are expected to wear their own clothes, clothing worn for serving should:

- Be comfortable and practical.
- Allow for free movement.
- Be hygienic.
- Look good to the customers and the member of staff.
- Blend with the atmosphere of the restaurant.
- Have strong pockets to hold note pads, cork screws etc.

A change of work clothes is necessary to allow for laundering. Daily washing of washable clothing is desirable.

✳ FOR INTEREST

In some restaurants where there is a particular theme, serving staff will be expected to wear make-up and clothes to reflect the correct image. Standards of cleanliness should still be maintained.

Shoes

Serving staff spend the major part of their working hours on their feet, so comfortable, practical shoes are a priority. It is important that shoes have a non-slip sole and heels are of a practical height. Open toes shoes should not be worn, in the event of an accident a sturdy pair of shoes will protect the feet from hot liquids and dropped plates.

Shoes should be kept clean and in good repair.

Personal attributes

Friendliness It is important to smile and be friendly, without being overly familiar with customers. Address customers by name, if known, or else by 'sir' and 'madam'. Be *respectful* rather than *servile*.

Courtesy Serving staff should be courteous and good mannered at all times, even when dealing with rude and unpleasant customers.

Speech Serving staff should be able to pronounce words properly and be able to talk to customers easily, without mumbling or shouting. Each member of the serving staff should be able to give an explanation of any terms on the menu.

Handwriting It is important to write legibly, both for the sake of the kitchen staff and cashier and for later reference to the order by the serving staff.

Memory It is useful to develop the skill of being able to remember which customer at which table gave an order, it will save time and give a good impression to the customer.

Checklist on customer skills

- Smile.
- Avoid looking harassed.
- Avoid peculiarities of dress or behaviour.
- Do not stare at customers, but keep an eye on the tables.
- Walk quickly, but without undue haste.
- Do not start conversations with customers, but respond when they talk to you.
- Avoid arguments or loud conversations with other staff members when in the restaurant.
- Treat all customers the same, do not show favouritism because of the likelihood of a large tip.
- Never discuss customers or staff members with other customers.
- Respond quickly when the customer signals for attention, by waving or making a slight head jerking movement.

 REMEMBER

The *rules* of dress can be summarised as:

Neat	Sensible
Clean	Safe
Well pressed	Comfortable
Practical	

A lot of *jewellery* should be avoided, it will get in the way when serving, will distract customers and may be unhygienic.

 TO DO

Write a short report on two recent eating out experiences, one you enjoyed and one you did not. List as many of the points as you can which made the one good and the other bad. Note which of these were due to the attitudes and behaviour of the serving staff, how they looked, what they said (or failed to say).

In order to provide customers with the standard of service they expect, it is important that serving staff are efficient in their methods of working. Serving staff who are punctual, helpful and aware of the needs of the customers will greatly contribute to the smooth running of the restaurant and the customers' enjoyment of the meal.

Working as a team

Each member of the serving staff is dependent on others for the successful completion of tasks. The organisation of the staff team will depend on the size and type of restaurant. A small restaurant may only have a staff of two carrying out all the necessary duties, from cooking the food to taking the payment. Large hotels may employ 100 staff, each of whom is responsible for a different task.

However large the restaurant, a helpful positive attitude towards other members of staff is more likely to achieve the desired results.

Timing

One of the most valuable skills to be learnt in food service is that of being able to time the progression of the meal so that customers do not feel they are being rushed, nor do they feel they have been forgotten.

1. Serving staff should be able to estimate the time it will take to serve the meal and for customers to eat it.
2. Serving staff should be familiar with food preparation times, so that courses can be served appropriately staggered to minimise delays, and so that all customers at one table are served with a course at the same time.

Punctuality

Serving staff have a responsibility both to other members of staff and the customers to be punctual. If a member of staff turns up late for duty, other staff members will have to cover for them, causing delay and resentment.

Coping with pressure

When the restaurant is very busy, several tables may require serving at the same time. Panicking will not achieve faster or more efficient service.

Apologise to the customers for any delay, attempt to estimate how long they will have to wait and assure them they have not been forgotten.

Timing of service

- Serve the first course as soon as possible after taking the order.
- Inform customers if there is going to be a delay.
- Keep an eye on the table, top up wine glasses, bring more bread and butter.
- Clear a course as soon as it is obvious that everyone has finished eating (usually when knives and forks are placed together on the plate).
- Take the dessert order promptly after clearing the main course.
- Suggest coffee and liqueurs after the dessert has been cleared.
- Present the bill when requested or when it is apparent that the customers have finished the meal. Leave the table.
- Return after a few minutes to take the payment.

Avoiding wastage

Working efficiently includes avoiding wastage, serving staff should ensure that:

- All appliances are turned off when not in use to save gas and electricity.
- While meanness is avoided, there is no unnecessary waste of food.

Catering for customers with special needs

Serving staff may be required to cater for blind or disabled people, the aim being to maintain as normal a service as possible, while paying consideration to the needs of the customers.

1. **Elderly people**

   - There must be easy access to their table.
   - An upright chair may be required.

2. **Blind customers**

   - There must be easy access to their table.
   - They should be placed at a table where they will not have to move for other customers.

3. **Deaf customers**

   - They should be placed where they can see everything.
   - They should be placed where there are even noise levels, away from the stereo or telephone.
   - Listen carefully to the customer's voice, it may not be very clear.

4. **Customers in wheelchairs**

   - Easy access to the table is essential.

5. **Catering for children**

   - Give the child a high chair or cushion to sit on.
   - Place the child where it is possible to see what is going on.
   - Seat the family where noise will cause the least disturbance to other customers.

 TO DO

Breakfast is a meal where speed is often the most important aspect of timing. Make a list of all the steps that can be taken to ensure the meal service is fast, noting the points where good timing is required by the serving staff.

Serving staff have a responsibility in ensuring that safe and hygienic standards are kept in the restaurant.

Safety in the restaurant

Safety means preventing accidents that can harm staff or customers. Serving staff can help to prevent accidents by:

1. Observing and following closely all required work procedures, for example, by properly completing cleaning tasks.
2. Keeping the work areas in a safe condition, for example, by removing all used plates to the wash-up area as soon as possible, rather than letting dirty crockery pile up on the sideboard.
3. Reporting any problems requiring repair and maintenance as soon as they are observed, for example, a rip in the carpet or a loose tile on the floor.
4. Notifying supervisors immediately of any accident, however slight.

Common accidents in a restaurant and how to prevent them

Burns and scalds	● treat hotplates and gas or spirit lamps carefully to avoid burns. ● keep handles turned away from busy areas. ● use dry cloths to hold hot plates.
Falls	● keep floor areas clean and dry. ● remove all hazards, such as dirty linen, off the floor. ● open and shut doors carefully. ● walk, don't run. ● wear sensible shoes on duty.
Cuts	● take care when using knives. ● keep sharp articles away from serving areas. ● clear up broken glass or china immediately.

Take special care when using electrical equipment, ensure that hands are dry, switch off and unplug the equipment when it is not in use.

Hygiene in the restaurant

The serving staff's responsibility for hygiene does not end with their own personal hygiene, not does the need for proper sanitary procedures end once the food has been prepared.

Hygienic procedures include:

- Covering food before and during service. This avoids contamination by dust, insects and from sneezing or coughing.
- Keeping cold food refrigerated until required for service.
- Avoiding the use of hotplates to heat food; they should only be used to keep hot food hot.
- Serving food promptly to customers once it is ready.
- Cleaning up any split food as soon as the spill occurs.
- Using separate serving utensils for different food items, and a clean set each time a dish is served.
- Always holding cutlery by the handle and not touching the eating surface.
- Always holding crockery by the rim.
- Always holding glasses by the stem or base.
- Never re-using food that has been served to customers but not consumed, for example leftover bread rolls.
- Practising sanitary personal habits; serving staff should not smoke, eat, chew, sneeze, cough or otherwise practise bad habits in the dining or kitchen areas.

Unavoidable accidents

Even when all obvious precautions have been taken, an accident may still occur. It is therefore important for staff to know what to do in the case of an accident.

1. **Knowledge of first aid** Immediately after an accident has occurred, first aid is the primary concern. In most establishments one of the staff members will be properly trained. A first aid kit should be available in the restaurant and all members of staff should be aware of where it is kept. If information on the basic treatment of common accidents, such as burns and scalds, is displayed, become familiar with it.
2. **Fire** Service staff should know where fire extinguishing equipment is located and how to use it. In large establishments fire drills will ensure that staff are aware of exits and are sure of their roles in aiding customers to leave the premises. Staff working in small restaurants should sort out an action routine in the event of a fire.

Any accident should be reported to the supervisor immediately. A clear statement of the events leading to the accident should be recorded, usually on a special form or in the accident book.

> **‼ REMEMBER**
>
> - Any cleaning tasks which are the responsibility of the serving staff should be thoroughly carried out, both from the point of hygiene and safety.
> - Floor areas should be kept clean and dry at all times.
> - Table tops must be kept spotless; dirty cleaning cloths should never be used.
> - Waste should be collected and placed in easily cleanable containers in a safe position.
> - Cutlery should be carefully stored in racks or drawers with the handles facing in the same direction.
> - Cups and containers used for serving or eating food should never be used to store or hold other substances, for example disinfectants and solvents.

>   **TO DO**
>
> Make a list of safety and hygiene procedures that are carried out at your place of work or at a restaurant of your choice. How often are the tasks carried out? Can you think of any improvements?